# The Role of Parents in Education

## How to Raise an Educated Child Using Highly Effective Parent Involvement Activities

**Frank Dixon**

Before we begin, I have something special waiting for you. An action-packed 1 page printout with a few quick & easy tips taken from this book that you can start using today to become a better parent right now!

It's my gift to you, free of cost. Think of it as my way of saying thank you to you for purchasing this book.

**Claim your download of Profoundly Positive Parenting with Frank Dixon by scanning the QR code below and join my mailing list.**

Sign up below to grab your free copy, print it out and hang it on the fridge!

**Sign Up By Scanning The QR Code With Your Phone's Camera To Be Redirected To A Page To Enter Your Email And Receive INSTANT Access To Your Download**

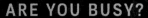

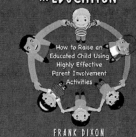

Before we jump in, I'd like to express my gratitude. I know this mustn't be the first book you came across and yet you still decided to give it a read. There are numerous courses and guides you could have picked instead that promise to make you an ideal and well-rounded parent while raising your children to be the best they can be.

But for some reason, mine stood out from the rest and this makes me the happiest person on the planet right now. If you stick with it, I promise this will be a worthwhile read.

In the pages that follow, you're going to learn the best parenting skills so that your child can grow to become the best version of themselves and in doing so experience a meaningful understanding of what it means to be an effective parent.

# Notable Quotes About

# Parenting

*"Children Must Be Taught How To Think,
Not What To Think."*

— **Margaret Mead**


**"It's easier to build strong children than to fix
broken men [or women]."**

**- Frederick Douglass**


**"Truly great friends are hard to find, difficult
to leave, and impossible to forget."**

**— George Randolf**


**"Nothing in life is to be feared, it is only to be
understood. Now is the time to understand
more, so that we may fear less."**

**— Scientist Marie Curie**

# Table of Contents

# Introduction

Every parent wants to see their child succeed in academics. They go to great lengths to ensure that their child is well-acquainted with all the necessary tools they need to learn. From fancy stationery to books and play, the early ages of a child's developmental years revolve around these. Getting a star on a test, a smiley face on the exam sheet from the teacher, and a treat at home to celebrate inclusion in the school's soccer team are all different ways we encourage learning and education.

However, what many parents forget while in the race to raise a topper is that every child learns differently. Different mediums and interests attract them. Different subjects influence their learning differently. For example, a child may struggle with math but be excellent at arts and crafts. A child may not do well with sports but be excellent in literature and poetry. With different interests comes different enthusiasm. When children feel motivated, they are more likely to pursue their interests with more conviction. With increased conviction comes success.

Since it all begins with how we pick up new things, process new information, and interpret and remember it, it is important to see how the brain learns something new. What is the process? Why do certain things stick, and certain things don't? Can children do as well as they do in subjects they don't like versus the ones they do like? These are all important questions to ask, and as parents who want to get more involved in their child's education, we must find the answers together.

Children come into this world with strong educational instincts. They are naturally inquisitive, playful, social, and attentive to all that's happening around them. They have an innate desire to grow up and do what grown-ups do. Without any effort and essentially no instructions, they learn to walk on their own, climb, and jump. They pick up words, learn a new language from scratch, argue, annoy, amuse, befriend, and seek answers to their curiosities. They watch, listen, and explore, having the chance to acquire an enormous amount of information about their physical and social world. Through unstructured play, they hone their skills that foster physical, social, intellectual, and emotional growth.

They do all this before they start school or through any systematic way. They do it by watching you.

They engage their senses and mind together. They pick up habits, accents, and vocabulary from you. You are their primary role model—even before they begin school.

Your role is the main role. You aren't the side character. You play the lead.

Therefore, you need to get more involved, engaged, and interested. You need to provide your guidance every step of the way so that they can become successful adults and excel in their lives, academics, and careers.

In this book, we discuss the strategies and practices that offer you a chance to be more engaged and involved with your children and their education. We look at how you can be a role model for them.

# Chapter 1:

# What Is Parent

# Involvement?

From potty training to making them eat vegetables, parents are responsible for all the learning during the early stages of a child's life. The day they board the bus to school for the first day is the day when parents finally breathe a sigh of relief. Now the responsibility of educating them is handed onto someone else— someone who is more qualified than them to ensure that the child receives the education they need.

There are two things wrong with that thought. First, it isn't a sigh of relief but rather worry that grips their core. They are sending off their kid to a place they haven't been to before. They don't know if they will make friends or spend the whole day crying or sitting in a corner. Second, no matter what anyone tells you, no one can be a better guide, teacher, and mentor for your child than yourself.

In fact, the role of parents in the education of their children increases when they start school. Research shows that parental engagement in education results in greater academic success and increased confidence (PTA, 2000). With parental involvement, children feel supported and loved. Completing homework together isn't just an act of engagement but rather a connection. With healthy parenting, parents can develop a lifelong love for learning.

Encouraging parents to become more involved in their child's education is more than just a need. It proves to be one of the best ways to provide a positive learning environment for every child. It can help parents learn about their child's learning ability and style better. With that knowledge, they can share their ideas and thoughts on a subject more engagingly and interactively.

# Understanding Parent Involvement

Experts believe that parental involvement is the sharing of responsibility between the parent and teacher to help children meet their educational goals and excel with promising success. Parental involvement takes place when parents become involved in school events and meetings, as well as willingly volunteer to show their support at home and school. It involves an act of commitment they make to ensure that their child receives the best learning and education. It shows that parents prioritize their child's education. It prompts educators to listen and provide every child space to think freely and learn as per their skills and competence.

Parental involvement in school is different from parental engagement; however, both serve the same goal. The idea is to encourage participation by the parents in their child's school activities and academics. When parents and teachers work together, they can provide the child an environment for healthy mental stimulation and growth which will help them ace their grades. Parents and teachers aren't simply mentors; they also take on the role of advisors and guide children to set high but realistic educational goals. Since every child is unique and learns differently, paying attention offers them to pick things at their own pace and time.

It won't be wrong to say that a parent's involvement in their child's education can help them become better advisors on their child's behalf. Many children with learning problems and disabilities remain quiet or unaware of their struggles. Teachers assume that the child isn't showing interest in their studies. However, this isn't the case with a learning disability. Children with learning disabilities require more assistance with speech and writing. Unlike other children, they need more time and explanation to interpret things. The sooner a learning disability is recognized, the earlier parents can start with intervention programs. Since parents spend the most time with their children, they are more likely to pick on the disability and talk to their child's respective educators.

# How Does My Involvement Affect My Child's Learning and Success?

Parental involvement has many benefits on your child's success. Many research studies are attesting to this. For instance, in one study, researchers compared the results of children with engaged parents and children without engaged parents and found that children with engaged parents scored higher on test results (Fan & Chen, 2001). In another study, researchers found that children with involved parents were more likely to graduate from high school and attend post-secondary education (Henderson & Mapp, 2002). This suggests an increased opportunity of landing a better, more high-paying job.

Researchers also believe that the more involved parents are in their child's life, the more confident and motivated they seem (Wairimu et al., 2016). They seem readier than most to take on new challenges and well-equipped to handle mishaps. They also appear more active and confident in the classroom. Parental involvement has also been linked with better social skills and classroom behavior. Children who feel supported and loved by their parents have more friends and have better etiquette. Furthermore, they are less likely to suffer from issues of poor self-esteem, require little to no redirection in the classroom, or have behavioral issues (El Nokali et al., 2010).

Across 50 different studies, monitored by a team of researchers, it was found that there is a strong link between family involvement and academic achievement (Hill & Tyson, 2009). The more involved a family is, the more effective they are in raising the child. Parents who are involved in their child's learning during their elementary school phase build a strong foundation for success and future engagement opportunities (Dearing et al., 2006).

Several studies also attest to the fact that involved parents decrease chronic absenteeism (Sheldon & Jung, 2015). Children whose parents pay attention to their education miss less than 20 days of school annually.

Better adaptation to school is another advantage for students who change schools often. The transition appears easier for them to make the switch and get accommodated properly. These students also report a greater sense of personal competence. They have efficacy for learning and are more drawn to school festivities and activities. They will actively volunteer to be a part of important social issues like anti-bullying campaigns, planting trees, or spreading awareness against racial prejudice. It is possible because parental involvement leads to greater self-satisfaction, control, social adjustment, and self-direction (Desforges & Abouchaar, 2003). Children who feel backed by their parents enjoy positive peer relationships, successful marriage, and limited delinquent behaviors.

Extensive research in student achievement also suggests that when parents get involved, there is a decrease in dropout rates among students. It also allows for a stronger connection between the parents and the teacher (Harris, 2005).

All these studies provide valuable insights on how parental engagement in education improves a child's chances of success. With better grades, increased participation in school activities, reduced absenteeism, and dropout rates, students are more likely to succeed and find themselves prospering careers. Add to that their increased self-confidence, self-direction, and satisfaction, and you have the recipe for a successful and happy adult.

**Chapter 2:**

# What Do Children Learn

# From Their Mothers and

# Fathers?

Having found a strong connection between academic success and parental involvement, one may wonder how to initiate learning and education at home. As parents are the primary teachers, the role they play in raising a sensible and educated individual is important. Therefore, in this next chapter, we look at how learning usually begins at home and what values and learning do mothers and fathers cultivate in their child's development.

Parents are the best educators as they provide children with knowledge in several ways. They are the ones who teach a child how to speak the language, pronounce words properly, and later, spell them correctly. They are the ones that instill core values and beliefs in them such as the difference between right and wrong; the importance of speaking truth, ethics, morals, and manners; etc. They teach them how to be respectful toward adults and affectionate toward children. They teach them how to behave in social gatherings, how to regulate emotions, and how to find their passions.

It is through their efforts that a child develops a unique personality and picks up a distinctive set of skills. It is their hard work that makes the child a desirable individual and adult. It is the values they instill that make them either admirable to others or admirable and intolerant. How they share and talk about love and relationships in the house becomes the foundation of how they perceive relationships in their life. If parents fail to provide children with a healthy home environment, they often end up raising a child that doesn't value family life and meaningful relationships.

Even though they mold a child's personality, interests, and passions from the very clay they are made from, science still puts more importance on the relationship a child shares with their mother.

## Many Say the Mother Is the First and Best Educator

According to Malcolm X (n.d.), "The mother is the first teacher of the child. The message she gives that child, that child gives to the world."

A mother is a life-giver. The bond shared between the child and the mother is forever unique. Therefore, more responsibility lies on her to be the child's sole educator. A child sees the mother as a trustworthy figure. They know that a mother will never want to harm the child. They know that a mother will be the first one to come to the aid when they need help. They know that she will protect them first and then herself.

The feeling of being a mother, to the woman, is more powerful. This is the same for every species. A mother always assures her child's life whether inside a home or in the wild—surrounded by wild animals. She will put her life in danger—many times sacrificing herself—to ensure that her offspring remains safe. She raises the child from when they can't speak or walk to when they reach total independence.

Since the connection is both biological and physiological, a mother represents the first and reasonable educator in her child's development and growth. She teaches her child about moral values, responsibilities, and acceptable behaviors. She teaches them about carrying themselves in society, how to make friends, and the importance of relationships and friendships. Through her, a child learns about respect, unconditional love, and what it means to take care of someone. Through her, a child learns how to put others first, be compassionate, and be grateful.

# What About Fathers?

This certainly doesn't mean that fathers never play a role in educating their children. However, when it comes to parenting, they are often made to feel like second best. Depictions of dads, whether in literature or popular culture, push the stereotype of fathers as emotionally disconnected, distant, and incompetent. They are shown as secondary parents and are pressured to take the back seat. Therefore, when it comes to active parenting, fathers feel less involved in the decisions regarding their child's basic needs like food, clothing, and homework.

Even when they try to play an active role in their child's life by being present and helping out with things like changing diapers or bathing the child, they are ridiculed among their friends and family. They are reminded that it isn't their role to play and that they can never do it as well as the mother does. Only recently have organizations started to consider a thing such as paternity leave. There was no concept of it a decade ago.

But, despite that, a father's role can't be underestimated. They do and must play an active role in their child's life, whether it's about fulfilling their basic needs or education. Their involvement is equally important in raising a healthy and happy child.

An active father increases a child's problem-solving skills. Active fathers ignite curiosity and exploration. They are the masters of DIY-ing things and finding unique ways to deal with common problems. This is crucial for a child's cognitive development as they learn about resilience. When they see that their father doesn't give up despite multiple failures, it boosts their self-confidence. They feel like they can take on challenges too. Children raised with active dads also score higher on math and verbal assessments. The presence of a strong father figure in the house also makes it less likely for a child to drop out of school or commit juvenile delinquencies.

Fathers also offer children, especially young boys, a positive role model to reinforce good behaviors and morals. It has been observed that children supervised by a powerful father figure have fewer impulse control and behavioral problems (Fagan & Palkovitz, 2007). They also have more gut and resilience along with longer attention spans. Children may also be more sociable and confident of their personalities when they have a strong parental figure to look up to in the form of a dad.

Some other studies also suggest that children brought up with a father in their lives are more generous and compassionate with an increased awareness of their rights and needs. This was particularly studied in a paper published in the *American Psychological Association Journal* (Stambor, 2005). It also looked at the changing roles of fathers in today's complex world. Today, fathers are expected to be more tuned in with their children and have increased meaningful interactions. They are expected to show more interest in their child's upbringing as well as education. There is also an emphasis on attending parent-teacher meetings and workshops designed for parents by school districts.

According to one study, fathers who respond to their infant's cries; hug and hold them often; and take an active part in their basic care like changing diapers or feeding have a long-lasting positive impact on their child's behavior and self-esteem (Sethna et al., 2017).

Young children, when praised by their fathers, feel like they can accomplish anything. Children, who are hugged and held more often, feel more comfortable and at ease in stressful times and are more likely to do well in school. They are also more like to stand against discrimination at school and advocate for others without being scared as opposed to those with uninvolved fathers.

## Diverse Roles Parents Play

Though their individual roles help shape a child's personality, imagine the impact it will have on their values and personality when parents come together and take joint interest in their education as a team. In today's world with busy lifestyles, one parent alone can't fulfill all the expectations. They both must take an interest and create a positive learning experience for their child in the house. Together, mothers and fathers can prevent children from deviating from the right path. Together, they can help them set realistic goals and remain focused on achieving them.

Children have gullible minds. When young, they aren't aware of the gravity of the impact their words, actions, and decisions have on their lives. They need role models and mentors to help them navigate their journey. This requires parents to wear many hats. Some days, they have to be a friend and get attuned with their life with friends; other days, they have to be a critic and prevent their child from making mistakes.

Let's explore these unique roles in detail and how a parent takes on them.

## A Guide

When young, children need help doing everything. They need to be shown how to carry, use, and handle things. From getting clothed to pouring cereal in their bowls, they need to be taught everything. This often requires patience, as they don't get it right the first or second time. Thus, parents must play the role of a guide that patiently tends to their every need and leads them by showing them how to do things. This also applies to guiding them on how to make friends, navigate social conversations, learn about personal hygiene, and a lot more things. A guide doesn't take over. They simply guide and then observe how the child is doing things independently.

## A Friend

A child's first friends are their parents and siblings. Before they go out and meet other people, their entire world is their parents. The bond they share is more than just a friendship. They are a friend that guides, helps, and shares love. They are a shoulder to cry on. They listen, advise, and collaborate. They share secrets. A parent should always be a friend first. They should make their children feel comfortable around them. They must ensure that the child isn't afraid. A certain level of openness and transparency must always be there between the parent and the child.

## A Teacher

A parent also takes on the role of a teacher, as it is through their eyes that the child sees the world. It is their guidance that allows them to explore their world safely. They set principles and expectations and help children at every step of the way in achieving them. They teach them about the world and everything in it. With their experience, they safeguard their children from making mistakes. They help children learn values, morals, and good behavior. As children grow older, parents help them with their schoolwork and facilitate them in preparing for tests and exams. They even offer to help with assignments and class projects.

## A Critic

A critic is someone that points out mistakes and shortcomings. They are people who notice what someone lacks and how they can improve. When it comes to parenting, all criticism must be constructive. This means that while parents offer their opinion, it shouldn't come off as a negative or belittling suggestion. The child shouldn't feel like a failure. Instead, it should motivate them and make them more excited to work harder and prove themselves. Therefore, when a parent takes on the role of a critic, they essentially offer help in the hopes of improving the child's confidence and effort. It isn't to put them down or make them feel hopeless.

## A Fitness Expert

Every child should reach age-appropriate milestones easily. They should have a healthy weight and height. They should exercise to stay active and keep their muscles in shape. The right guidance, from a parent, can help young minds build a healthy routine of incorporating exercise in their lives. Through them, they can learn about the importance of a good diet, sleep, and an active lifestyle. Parents can shape good exercising and nutrition habits in them, promoting a healthy relationship with food. However, this is possible through example. Parents must exercise and eat healthy themselves to ensure that their children pick up on the same practices.

## An Author

Parents are the greatest storytellers. Children learn various concepts about academics and life through stories. Stories about courage, honesty, challenges, and hardships are all lessons they pick from stories. Since kids love to hear stories, parents often share their life's wisdom and experiences in a story format. Whenever they want to impart wisdom about an emotional struggle their child is facing, they rely on their own experiences with it and how they overcome those struggles. Storytelling also inspires children to become storytellers themselves. They can master the art of emphasizing, piquing interest, and engagement by listening to stories.

## A Doctor

To be a doctor, you don't need to have studied medicine. There is so much more to it than just drugs and prescriptions—things like taking a hot water bath to relieve pain, getting some sleep to refresh the body, sipping on something hot during the flu, etc. Apart from that, there is the mental health of a child that requires equal prominence. Parenting helps children accept failures, overcome emotional challenges, understand self-discipline, and accept others for who they are. Mental well-being relies on being happy and surrounding yourself with happy and positive thoughts. Acceptance, gratitude, and mindfulness are all important aspects of it, and only a parent can teach them well.

## A Spiritual Guru

Finally, a parent also takes on the role of a spiritual guru that teaches children about their religion, culture, and spirituality. It is a parent that teaches children to be empathetic, hold ethical values, value honesty, modesty, and courage. It is them that liberate a free spirit in kids. Parents teach children to be more accepting of who they are. They teach them to see the good in others and believe in the greater good. They teach them to have a sense of purpose in life and be driven by it.

# Chapter 3:

# Get Involved in School

The key to parental involvement in education is coordination. Parents and teachers must work together to help children establish high-level goals and achieve them. This requires effective communication between school and home. An ideal channel of communication should encompass every stakeholder in the mix such as the parents, teachers, administrators, club leaders, coaches, and policy makers. Parent-teacher organizations (PTOs), along with policy makers, must devise strategies that help parents become more involved and engaged in their child's education.

A strong school culture cultivates a thriving community where the student, parent, and teacher have easy access to each other and have the opportunity to trigger positive change. When parents and teachers connect, they can become more aware of their child's unique learning styles, their progress, and their annual goals. They can talk about the many interests that the child has or areas that they are exceptionally well in. Similarly, they can also identify the areas that need working and hone them. A school-wide open channel of communication ensures that critical information is conveyed in an accessible manner, and neither the child nor the parent feels left out.

As simple as it sounds, many challenges prevent this communication from taking place. Before we discuss the many strategies that can increase parental engagement in schools, let's have an overview of these barriers to communication between the school and parents.

# Parents and Teachers: Need for Collaboration

It is said that it takes a village to raise a child. An important aspect of successful upbringing involves a child's education. Education doesn't necessarily involve literature, math, and science. Education is the process of gaining new information. This information can come from learning a new skill, reading a book, or learning through experience. Education teaches us about moral values, different cultures, people, ethnicities, countries, and much more. It teaches us about social norms and how to live like sensible and law-abiding citizens. It teaches us how to communicate and be respectful. It teaches us about spirituality, the need for purpose in life, and goal-setting. Education allows us to become better people.

Children learn best when everyone around them, especially the significant adults in their lives, works together in supporting and encouraging them. This principle should serve as a guide when we think about how schools should engage parents in education. This principle also helps us set parameters on how to teach children. Since schools can't address all the developmental needs of a child alone, the meaningful interaction between the parents and school can help in raising intelligent and cultured adults.

The need for strong partnerships between families and schools may seem like common sense. Isn't it the best way to educate a child? In simpler times, the relationship is natural and easy to maintain. Teachers and parents were often neighbors. They could easily share their concerns, talk about the child's progress, and tutor the child if needed out of a friendly relationship. Parents and teachers shared the same message with the child, and the child knew what was expected of them in terms of learning and behavior.

Today's society is more complex and demanding. Neither parents nor educators have enough time to get to know each other, let alone establish a working relationship. They may greet one another on the way to school when the parent drops off the child or when they are invited to a parent-teacher meeting. In many communities, the parents feel discouraged going up to a teacher or spending time in classrooms. Parents feel that educators only consult a family member when the child is in trouble. This often results in mistrust, misunderstanding, and a lack of respect. So, whenever a child fails, the parents blame the educator, and the educator blames the parents.

Another barrier is artificial distinctions we have created in our minds. We believe that parents and teachers have a distinct role to play. Teachers and schools are expected to stick to academics whereas parents are expected to teach morals and emotional development at home. This is impossible because when a child enters the classroom, they meet children from all backgrounds, cultures, and ethnicities. They all bring different values and morals. When the child befriends them, they learn different morals and values from them. They observe each other's lifestyles and imitate them. They notice how one makes and executes decisions and solves problems and picks up on those habits.

When they go home to their parents and community, they learn different values. All these help shape their personality and help determine their self-worth, competence, and understanding of the world.

Then, there is also the case of diversity in living arrangements. Not every child has the same social status. They come from different homes and are living different lifestyles. Family dynamics are also an issue these days, as many children are being raised by single parents.

Some families move a lot, too. This prevents the child and their educators from forming a connection where they can help each other out. Parents also have a difficult time with this change in school and education systems.

For teachers, there is also a language and cultural barrier. Today, schools enroll students from different backgrounds that speak different languages. For a teacher to deal with an immigrant parent is more challenging than dealing with a parent born and raised in the same country. The values and policies are similar, and it's easier to lay down expectations.

Lack of accessibility, as previously talked about, is another challenge. Not all schools are equipped with computers or staff competent at using them for purposes other than email, especially the ones in smaller towns and counties. They lack software and programs that offer a duly report card or test results. This leaves parents in the dark about their child's progress throughout the year.

For parents, appropriate communication tools are also a barrier. A child may have five to six different teachers, each using a different communication medium to get in touch with the parents. Some may prefer one-on-one interactions while others are more comfortable via messages, phone, or email. Navigating these multiple communication channels can leave a parent feeling overwhelmed and frustrated. Then, some teachers may also use buzzwords that parents of today don't resonate with. For this very reason, they avoid any form of contact with their child's educator.

# Getting Started

So how can one improve this communication between the school and parents? What strategies can parents and teachers use to improve how information gets received? How can parents get more involved, and how much involvement does the school allow? Let's have a look below.

Attend back-to-school events or orientation programs that schools host every year to allow parents to get more engaged in their child's education. These programs are designed specifically for parents so that they can know their child's teachers at the beginning of the school year. These events also provide other families to meet and interact. Apart from this, many schools also hold parent-teacher conferences and meetings monthly or bi-annually to discuss each child's progress and grades. These help parents and teachers to be on the same page with what expectations they have from the child and how they will work together on accomplishing them.

As a parent, ask your child's teacher the best way to communicate. Inquiring about their preferred channel of communication will help you stay up to date about your child's progress. It will also exhibit your devoted interest in your child's welfare—something that many educators appreciate. In case a problem arises, the same channel can be used to address it promptly.

Demonstrate a positive relationship with learning at home. Go book shopping together, schedule time for playing out characters from your child's favorite book, and DIY flashcards with new words to increase their vocabulary. If a child learns something new without feeling like they are made to learn about it, your strategy is successful. Once your child starts to show interest in their studies, they will begin to show more interest in school as well. They will become more confident with that extra knowledge they have and use that to educate others as well.

Whenever your child participates in a talent show, exhibition, or fair, make sure to show up to offer support and encouragement. Attending school-wide events allows you to stay in touch with your child's extracurricular activities as well as their coaches, trainers, and teachers. You can be at the forefront and help your child master their unique talents and passions by being an active part of their journey.

Whenever you have an upcoming parent-teacher conference, go prepared with your questions and concerns. Don't feel shy in expressing your opinions in case the child reports a bad interaction. Think of three to five issues that you want to raise awareness about with the teacher as well as school administration. Confidently suggest different methodologies if you believe your child can learn better. Note down all the things and suggestions the teacher recommends. Talk about your child's future goals as well as how you can work as a team to help them accomplish them.

Volunteer at your child's school. Many schools ask for extra workers and volunteers who will help out with the arrangements and organization of an event. For example, you can offer chaperone trips and school dances for all the students in your child's class. You can offer your writing skills to the school administration and prepare press releases, campaigns, and proposals. You can also translate newsletters into different formats or languages. You can assist with the planning of an event and handle phone calls to let other parents know about the event or materials their child needs to bring to school. You can cater at a fundraising event such as a bake sale. You can organize lunches or monitor school practices. You can join a specific club or interest group. If you are skilled at art or language, you can help children who take interest in learning it. If you are into fitness and sports, you can assist coaches and gym teachers. You can supervise, speak in the classroom on career day, or judge experiments at a science fair.

Finally, you must show interest in your child's school and homework. Parents who are actively engaged in their child's education can notice areas in which the child struggles. They are in a good position to offer support and guidance. Helping children with homework also communicates care and affection. Showing concern about what they are learning at school helps reinforce the importance of it as well. This has been elaborately discussed in the next chapter where we explore different tips and practices to help you get more involved in your child's education.

**Chapter 4:**

# Homework and

# Assignments

The many hours children spend at school and the amount of attention they receive from their teachers is limited. Therefore, teachers need assistance and support from parents and families to understand a child's learning style, their learning ability, and the pace at which they learn best. This knowledge allows them to impart new information in a better and specific way. With homework and assignments, they can assess a child's learning style and capacity and also learn about whether the child is offered help by the parent or not. When parents get more involved in homework, it shows. It shows when a child confidently brings up their homework to the teacher's desk, knowing they have done everything right.

Homework has been a part of every child's life since the beginning of a formal school setting. Homework encourages exploration and thinking. Most of the time, assignments are based on the knowledge a child learned acquired during class. Homework tells the teacher whether they were successful in imparting new knowledge or not. Homework helps children develop positive study habits. It encourages them to use their time well, build interest in learning, and be accountable for their actions (work).

Helping young children with homework has many benefits for the whole family. For the child, it can provide opportunities to learn new things and be creative. For parents, it serves as a bonding time with their child. Together, they can both improve their learning and knowledge about the world.

The importance of parents engaging in their child's learning and education is invaluable. Helping with schoolwork is an important responsibility. It promotes and supports the learning process. When parents bring their experience and expertise, learning becomes priceless. Success in school is best predicted by how involved parents are with the child at home. Helping children with their homework develops their self-confidence. It encourages them to contribute to the classroom more confidently and actively. It also enables parents to share some meaningful time with their children and talk about their own experiences with learning, its benefits, and the best ways to develop the habit.

# Let's Talk Benefits

Further looking at the benefits, we come to notice that helping children with homework alleviates stress in them. Sometimes, even the simplest of problems appear challenging. Some children face difficulty in certain subjects or topics. When parents get on board, they can guide the child better with relevance and personal experience. They can make random content meaningful by adding a touch of their knowledge about it. This can help children grasp every subject.

A parent's involvement also improves subject and skill retention. Parents can get in more depth about a topic and allow children to hone their skills on a greater level. For example, if the child learns best through audio and visuals, they can turn a boring story into an interesting one by sketching the scenes or adding dramatic sound effects to it. Similarly, if a child has trouble remembering the names of different fishes in the sea, parents can plan a trip to the aquarium and have the child learn more about them. This way, not only will the child remember the names they had trouble remembering earlier but rather also learn about their distinct features and characteristics. This gaining of supplementary knowledge is only possible when a parent gets involved in their child's education and homework.

When a child knows about different topics in such great detail, they can confidently speak about them with their peers and educators, becoming a valuable resource. They can also improve their social skills by engaging more enthusiastically with other children in the classroom.

Since learning can be accelerated in the classroom, children may lack valuable, in-depth knowledge about things. When parents get involved in homework, they have more time to go into more detail about what the school failed to touch upon. As most schools have elaborative curricula and a small amount of time, this is unfortunately what happens. Luckily, with parents helping children with their homework, they can spend extra time building their knowledge about various topics.

Parental involvement also increases creativity and thinking skills. When parents take out the time to help children with their homework, they essentially create a positive environment that nurtures exploration and curiosity. This curiosity leads to out-of-the-box ideas and problem-solving skills. Children find their true passions and interests and devote more time to them.

With parental supervision, children can beat procrastination and remain focused and organized. They can learn to set priorities and work on their weaknesses. With some assistance and time from their parents, they can learn faster and better. Being organized helps them save time. Being focused allows for better grasping of information as one has a clear and devoted mind. It also enables children to set goals and achieve them in the designated time.

Finally, it can cultivate positive learning habits and behaviors in children. By reading together or doing projects as a team, children build a love for learning. They recognize that more knowledge is truly empowering. Good learning habits are lifelong skills.

# Tips for Helping Children With Homework

One school of thought believes that children must be made to do their work. Searching for the right answers and thinking critically are part of the process that increases their intelligence and thirst for knowledge. Therefore, holding the pencil and doing work for them doesn't make sense.

True, children must be encouraged to problem-solve themselves. However, sometimes they can't, and out of fear, they don't ask their parents. Confusion and lack of understanding, in this case, can deter one's mind and heart from the love of learning. They may begin to procrastinate or put off things. They may make excuses to avoid doing homework and lie to their teachers in the classroom. This isn't something we can allow either.

So how can we proceed? How can we ensure that the child retains their love for learning as well as do most of the thinking and working themselves? How can we tread around the thin line of giving them all control or taking it completely? Below are some interesting tips.

First up, you must establish a routine. Children and adults do well with structure and routine. Knowing when it's time to turn off the TV and open their bag gives them a heads-up. They can mentally prepare themselves for the task. Set a regular time for homework and revisions. Remind your child 15 minutes before the scheduled hour that they should put away all other things and take out their books and copies.

Next, designate a specific area for homework and assignments. Call it the homework-friendly area. Ideally, it should be a well-lit, distraction-free space with all the supplies like pencils, erasers, rulers, and paper within reach. There should be a rigid work surface to put down their copies on as well. Ensure that no external noises and sounds distract the child in the duration. If the TV is on, turn it off. Put away your phone, tablet, or laptop. If you have smaller children that interrupt and make noise, have them settled in the next room.

Once they are settled, ask your child about their day at school, what they learned about, and what homework their teacher gave them. Ask them to read it out loud so that the expectations are clear from the start. If there is confusion, inquire about how the teacher asked them to do it. Simply asking and revisiting the day's activities will help the child feel encouraged and attended to.

Let them begin the work themselves but remain focused on what they are doing. Don't point out their mistakes right away. Give them a chance to correct themselves. Direct them toward the right answer but don't just blurt it out. They need to figure it out themselves. If the answers require some research, surf the Internet, or go to a local library to get reference books for better comprehension. This can be a quicker and more engaging way to look for answers and build the habit of researching and exploring.

In case the child feels burned out, let them have some break time in between. You can eat some snacks or watch a short clip to distract them for a while. You need to avoid those feelings of failure and frustration from settling in because they can discourage the child from further learning.

If a child has trouble grasping a topic, use active learning techniques to connect it with the real world. Discuss with them the subjects they learn in school and how that knowledge can be applied in the real world. Provide examples using your everyday life and things happening around you, so they can remember it for later.

Always make sure to break down homework into manageable chunks on those heavy homework weekends. This will allow your child to tackle each separate chunk as a different task that ultimately leads to the end goal.

Finally, don't forget to praise their work and effort. Be open and expressive about their brilliance and intelligence with relatives. Speak about their achievements, and how proud they make you, in front of others. This will serve as motivation for future learning.

# Chapter 5:

# It's Time to Open a Book

Reading together as a family promises a host of benefits. According to the American Academy of Pediatrics, reading to children daily from infancy stimulates cognitive development and builds key language, social, and literacy skills (High, 2014). The lead researcher for the study, Dr. Pamela High, spoke about the benefits in detail. She believes that a six-month-old baby can learn to hold a book, a one-year-old can point out some of the illustrations, and by the time they reach toddlerhood, they may even point out alphabets or words. The experience of learning through reading is seated in the relationship between the child and the parent. Reading out loud to a child motivates them to work harder and become independent readers themselves.

Reading with children increases the time parents spend together. Suppose if a parent reads with their children for 20 minutes every day of the week, it comes down to more than 120 hours per year spent together. Imagine the number of new words your child is exposed to in that one year of reading—about 1.8 million! When children can confidently speak a language and have an excellent vocabulary, they can feel more confident in social surroundings such as at school and in the family.

Reading books with children also expands on the variety of words children use. Both fiction and nonfiction books contain many words we seldom use in our everyday life. Exposure to these builds the child's literacy skills (National Center on Early Childhood Development, Teaching and Learning, n.d.).

# The Incredible Benefits of Reading Together

Besides improving vocabulary and literacy skills, there are many other benefits associated with reading together as a family. For starters, more exposure and exploration aids education and learning. The more a child knows, the more intelligent they will be. The more intelligent they are, the more active and successful they will be in their professional lives. However, since success isn't the ultimate goal but rather developing the habit of reading in children, here's what your engagement and time can do for young minds.

## Emotional Togetherness

Through reading together, children can hone their listening and empathy skills. When parents and children explore new themes collectively, it offers a supportive and structured environment. In case the theme evokes strong emotions like reading about a national hero that died on duty, sharing that experience can cultivate empathy and gratitude in children. It can also teach them about resilience and gut. They can feel more confident dealing with their emotions and stress self-reliantly.

Emotional togetherness is an important need in today's time when devices have taken over our free time. Spending quality time reading with children can make them feel secure, loved, and valued (Duursma et al., 2008). Like you, they can also build a positive relationship with books and become lifelong readers.

**Encourage Imagination**

When parents open a book with a child, whether fiction or nonfiction, they are opening up a new world. Children learn about new cultures, people, and their stories. The more books they read, the more knowledge they gain. It is a lot like stepping into a different world. They can create their interpretations which boost creative thinking skills in them. They can create and visualize their own stories like what a character in their storybook looks like. All this imagination can come into play when they start school, and their knowledge span expands. According to a 2013 study, infants who are read to and talked to by their parents score higher in cognitive development, as well as analytical and language skills (Murray & Egan, 2013).

**Stronger Brain Development**

A child's brain continues to grow during the first five to seven years of their life. They learn to walk, talk, and move their arms and legs on their own. They learn an entirely new language just by listening to their parents and siblings. They understand basic instructions and can remember numbers on a list. This is all possible because of the conversations they hear. The more they hear, the more knowledge their brain processes. The more knowledge they gain, the more thoughtful and intelligent they grow up to be. Reading books with them is a great way to expose them to a wide range of words and ideas.

## Exposure to New Experiences

Many times, children feel afraid of encountering new situations alone—situations like the first day of the school year, making new friends, presenting in front of an audience, etc. These can lead to unwanted stress. Reading about such experiences in a book or story can mentally prepare them and hopefully ease the transition. Books are also a great way to expose children to many new situations like moving houses, going through a divorce, or living with a new parent. Knowing how to deal with stress and building resilience is what books can teach.

## Stress Relief

Reading for pleasure has been known to relieve stress and anxiety. It is an activity that requires focus and commitment. When you pick up a book, your mind becomes involved in the story, plot, and characters. This shift in your mentality is positive, as it can take your mind off everyday stresses. Reading with your child will offer them similar benefits. Children can get upset over small things and remain worried about them. Reading together can promise them a timely relief and a sense of enjoyment. Reading about how their favorite characters cope in stressful times also makes them courageous.

## Pleasurable Routine

Carving out time to read with your child, at the end of a busy and tiring day, can be a little breather everyone needs. Reading has also been linked with overall well-being such as lowered blood pressure and normal heart rate. According to research, it has the same effect on the body as humor or yoga (Rizzolo et al., 2011).

## Address Difficult Issues

For many parents, speaking about issues related to diversity, sexual orientation, and racial discrimination is difficult. They never build the courage to open up about them with their children. However, in today's time, it is becoming important that we encourage children to respect and accept people for who they are, regardless of where they come from or what they look like. Books can serve as a great medium to discuss such sensitive and controversial issues that feel uncomfortable otherwise. Together, you can read about different cultures and sexual orientations and later discuss about it. You can know their views about it and if needed, shape their thoughts to be more positive and accepting.

# How to Raise a Reader

We become lifelong readers for all sorts of reasons. Sometimes, it is a teacher that inspired us to read by assigning us a great book; sometimes, it is a random book we picked from a shelf during a trip to the library; sometimes, a book captured our imagination; and sometimes, it is a movie based on a book that we loved watching so much. All in all, it is the availability and encouragement from our teachers and parents that ignited this spark within us. Their appreciation and involvement in the activity of reading have helped us continue with our passion. Modeling good reading behaviors and habits has helped many children who were picky readers appreciate all forms of literature and writing.

Why not give our children the same opportunities? Why not help them pick the right books and read to them from an early age? Why not make them see reading as a pleasurable and joyous activity? If you want to raise a reader and help them excel in school, thanks to their vast knowledge and intelligence, here are some tips on getting started.

Read aloud. Many parents start to read to their children before their birth. Even though they might not understand a word or what the story is about, the tone and pitch of a parent's voice appear calming. Parents should start reading to their infants. There is nothing more adorable than having an infant on your lap or snuggled next to you, drifting off to sleep while you read. Early childhood reading experiences increase a child's observation and language skills. By looking at illustrations, shapes, and colors, they can learn to identify the differences earlier than most children.

Have plenty of books in the house. If you want to raise a reader, give them the resources they will need to become one. Make your house a book hub so that your child has something to pick every time they wish to read. Having books of different genres, colors, illustrations, and unique cover designs are all different ideas for a bookshelf. You can even DIY one with your child as a weekend project and let them decorate it with their favorite books.

Designate one corner in the house where all the reading happens. When growing up, children crave control and privacy. Having a special corner all to themselves for reading is a great way to keep them interested in reading. You can have them decorate it with murals, shelves, and their favorite stationery. You can also give them a journal to note their favorite quotes from a book and read them later together.

Pique interest by hooking them on a series. There are many excellent authors with multiple publications in a series. Take *Diary of a Wimpy Kid*, for example. As the central character overcomes new challenges in every other installment, it can be fun for children to be a part of that exciting journey. Reading books with sequels and installments keeps them hungry for the next one.

Find books that your child has an interest in. It doesn't always have to be fiction read. If your child is into arts, history, or cars, you can pick books that introduce them to the core concepts of things. For example, if they are into history, learning about pirates, the Vikings, and renowned explorers like Christopher Columbus is a great start.

Get in touch with your local library and inquire if they offer any weekend or monthly programs for young readers. Many libraries host small events every once in a while for young readers. Taking your child to them will encourage them to read, too. While there, make sure to get your child their library card. Children love to have something with their name on it. With a library card, they can borrow books and exchange them for new ones once they are done reading. Schedule trips to the library with enthusiasm and let your child pick a book of their choice using that library card.

Finally, be a role model. Kids are always watching us. If they see us picking up a book or enjoying a read on a Sunday morning, they are going to develop the same habits. If they see you fall in love with books, they will, too. Therefore, make sure to give them many glimpses of yourself reading. They should see it as an activity that brings joy and happiness. Discuss with them stories you read in a magazine or novel and how much you enjoyed it.

# Chapter 6:

# Trips, Trips, Trips

In modern-day life, it can be quite challenging for parents to schedule out time for their children. Hectic work schedules, work commitments, house chores, mental stress, etc. can all take a toll on one's routine, leaving little time for the whole family to bond and spend time together. They fear their children will become distant, and to counter that, they plan a family night for the weekends. However, you never know when something urgent comes up or you spend the whole day at Walmart shopping for essentials.

By the time you come home, you feel too drained to enjoy anything, let alone do something exciting. Since your involvement in their education and school comes recommended and backed by countless studies, there is something you can do that will tick all the boxes:

- Spending family time together

- Getting involved in your child's educational development

- Doing something fun and interesting

*An educational trip!*

An educational trip can be an interesting escape from the usual family nights at restaurants and play areas. It promises a wide range of opportunities to spend time together as a family as well as stay connected with your child's education. Educational trips for the family can teach children about new things and create authentic and unique experiences for children. Even a short trip to the park can be educational, as children can learn social skills and gain knowledge about traffic rules, road safety, etc. during the trip. A trip to the museum can be both exciting and informational. Children can learn about their country's history, cultural values, and meet their heroes.

Educational trips are an indispensable chance to create beautiful memories as well. They allow parents to teach children about the real world—something they can rarely learn about within four walls. Beyond the adventure each educational place promises, children can discover new hobbies and find their passions. For instance, a child may take up stamp collecting after getting inspired by the currency in old times.

# Importance of Educational Trips

Furthermore, family trips help children and parents break out of their routines and become a part of something creative and educational. It can help them unwind and chill out. Educational trips make children more inquisitive about the world. The more curious they become, the more knowledgeable they will become. They will voluntarily research more about their favorite subjects and areas of interest online and offline. They will be more enthusiastic to read books and question more. Apart from that, you can't ignore the following benefits.

Educational trips with the family expose children to new cultural experiences. They can learn about different worlds, people, and cultures first-hand. It opens their minds and eyes to new environments that shape their perspective. The more broad-minded and exposed they are to the real world, the better their take on current issues and social causes around them. Their exposure can someday lead to bigger and impactful ideas that can change the world. It also serves as a means to build empathy and compassion for others. For instance, they can learn about the struggles of the Black community throughout history and become an active advocate for equal rights for them. They can learn about the struggles of the LGBTQ+ community and raise awareness for them.

Educational tours and experiences are better at grabbing the attention of a student that doesn't take interest in studies otherwise. Learning about things firsthand can serve as a unique learning experience for them. Visual knowledge precedes what's written in books. Besides, classroom learning is often limited in terms of exposed sensors present in the outside world. If you have a picky learner, planning educational trips can be a great way to pique interest. They can learn and enjoy being on the trip. For instance, going to a planetarium can teach children about the solar system in a way that books can't. They are more likely to remember the experience forever.

Educational trips also become a source of invaluable information. The experience goes beyond reading about something. When students can witness what they are learning about, participate, and manipulate it, they believe more. Many schools plan trips to fields and farms to teach children about cattle and farming and how that contributes to everyday eating. When they see the whole process through their eyes, they can formulate their thoughts about it as well. Similarly, when they go on a trip with the family and observe the same, they can even participate in activities that they only read about in a book. For example, reading about milking a cow on a farm is more challenging than reading about it in a book.

Educational trips are also a source of entertainment for the whole family. Breaking away from normal routines helps children become more active and focused after returning from the trip. A trip combines learning and fun. Children can meet other kids their age, interact with people with interesting stories, and increase their knowledge base. After returning from the trip, they can talk about it more passionately with their peers and teachers.

Finally, with educational trips, children can be a part of worlds they can only read about within the four walls of the school. For example, they can explore the underwater world or swim with the dolphins during a diving session. They can visit an aquarium and see how fish live harmoniously in the ecosystem. If they are a fan of movies, you can take them to a theater and watch a live-action play of their favorite storybook. They can learn about filmmaking, how to set the stage, and how to direct scenes. These kinds of exposures can be extremely healthy and allow children to expand on the knowledge they gain at school. This form of interaction is a unique and unforgettable one.

# Ideal Places That Promise an Unforgettable Experience

Having already discussed most of the places on various occasions in the chapter, here's a brief of some amazing educational places you can enjoy going to as part of a family.

## Historical Places

Places like museums, historical buildings, and historical artifacts and structures are amazing places to begin exploring your country's rich history. There are numerous places in the U.S. alone that one can visit with children. From Lincoln Memorial to Independence Hall, from the Statue of Liberty to Yellowstone National Park in Wyoming, from Mark

Twain House to Yosemite National Park… many places are full of our country's diverse history. In the museums, you can find many artworks by famous people, remnants of important historical figures, and scriptures they left behind. Children can find it both fascinating and informational.

## Zoo

If your child loves wildlife and nature, there is no place better than visiting a local zoo. Zoos allow children to study and observe different animals from all over the world. Thankfully, there is signage and boards that talk about each animal's unique features and characteristics. This allows children to know about their habitats, lineage, and much more.

## National Park

National parks are a great place for a family picnic on the weekend. From fresh air to wide beautiful spaces, national and botanical parks offer families a great time to spend together. By being outdoors, children can get active, play around, and learn about different plants and animals.

## Aquarium

Going to the aquarium can be a cool experience for young children. They can immerse themselves in aquatic life and experience what it's like underwater. They can observe fish they only read about in books or watch in movies in real life. How often is it to see a shark, stingrays, or jellyfish up close? Although your child's school might have already taken them on a trip to the aquarium, going with your children is still special. They can see families of different varieties of fish living together and share a unique bonding experience.

**Farm**

Going to the countryside and spending a few days in a barn or farm is another experience you might want to share with your children. Raising chickens, looking after cattle, and riding horses are all activities that children can enjoy. They can also learn about how farmers live their lives, their daily work, how they raise animals, feeding them, and how they take care of them. On a vegetable or fruit farm, they can learn how to grow plants, the best seasons to grow them, and how to prevent crops from going bad. Many farming families also allow participants to tour their farm and witness how they process food, sort it, and send it to local shops. Learning about how meat, fruits, and vegetables make their way to a grocer's shelf can make children appreciate the work and workers. It can develop gratitude in them for being able to afford fresh food and enjoy it.

# Chapter 7:

# Promote Active Learning

Sensory-motor experiences involve feeling, hearing, smelling, listening, and looking at objects. Infants see the world through their eyes, hear their parent's voices, and use their hands and feet when making demands. When holding something in their hands, they use their eyes, hands, and mouths to have a sense of what it is. This is a form of active learning. Active learning allows parents to offer children the choice of what they want to do by providing them with opportunities to select their goals, materials, and interests.

It happens when we impart new information using objects, events, and stories. For example, if they want to learn about golfing, taking them to a golf course and letting them take a shot is active learning. We provide the child with the opportunity to learn something new by not only witnessing it live but also by being an active part of it. Since learning requires the presence of mind, focus, and dedication, it is often difficult for students to remain engaged, especially when learning about something uninteresting. Take learning about a historical figure, for example. A child might not be as interested in reading about Abraham Lincoln in a book as they would be while watching a movie based on the same character. Active learning demands that both the teacher (parent, in this case) and the child participate equally in the process of learning.

Active learning allows children to utilize imaginary and real-life situations by being present in them. It is what allows the young mind to develop distinct perspectives about things and learn through experience. Active learning is crucial in today's world when books are becoming obsolete, and teacher-student relationships are changing. Today, schools rely more on visual aids to enrich the experience of learning. As parents, we must bless our children with a similar experience where they learn about new things without feeling forced.

# Effectiveness of Active Learning

Active learning is a concept based on the theory of constructivism. It stresses the fact that we learn by constructing and building our understanding and perspectives. It is true since we can all develop different perspectives about certain things. For example, some people love the sound and smell of rain while others only see it as a nuisance that gets everything wet and muddy. These differences in opinions about the same natural phenomenon are a testament that our beliefs and perspectives shape our learning and thought processes. Following the same theory, learners also increase their existing knowledge to understand things more deeply. They use their analytical and critical thinking skills to evaluate and synthesize ideas based on their opinions and beliefs.

When children are allowed to understand things on a deeper level through active learning approaches, their learning experiences improve. Their interaction becomes more meaningful. Active learning fosters deep learning.

The theory of social constructivism (Berkeley Graduate Division, 2019) by social constructivist Lev Vygotsky further explores the subject of active learning and proposes that learning happens through social interactions with others. In his theory, he talked about the interaction between a teacher and a student. He developed the idea of the Zone of Proximal Development that lies between what a student can learn on their own and what a student can learn with their teacher's assistance and guidance. Qualified teachers focus learning activities in this zone. They offer guidance and support that improves the quality of learning for the student.

There are reasons why this works. The power of active learning is evident through studies, as it allows children to construct meanings of things and link new information with what they previously knew. It helps parents to understand that a child may know something but not apply that set of facts to a current problem. For example, if a child is stressed and knows of healthy coping strategies like deep breathing, meditation, and mindfulness, then why don't they apply them?

Active learning also tells parents what information is more transferable and what isn't. They can use this knowledge to analyze how to incorporate active learning in ideas that are complex to understand. It tells parents what their child's preferred learning style is. Some children enjoy the company of others when they are learning something new while others prefer to be alone. If you have multiple children in the house, knowing this can help you carve special one-on-one time for your child.

# Connecting Learning to Real Life

When we talk about active learning, there are several approaches that parents can incorporate. They can use inquiry-based learning that involves including children in the process of planning, investigating, and finding solutions together. This allows for teamwork and collaboration where the child feels free to communicate and be creative.

Active learning can also happen through play. Here, you allow the child to engage actively and imaginatively with objects, people, and their surroundings to build important social and life skills. An activity like gardening is an example. The child learns about seeds, how to plant them, what to water them, and where to place them for best exposure to sunlight.

A third approach is an event-based approach where children can plan and enact events based on their knowledge and experience. Role-playing characters from their favorite storybook and enacting the scenes is an example of active learning based on the event-based approach.

Similar activities for young children to engage in active learning involve the following:

## Building Blocks

You may think of building blocks as a random activity, but it introduces children to complex concepts like spatial relationships, weight and balance, relative size, and problem-solving. They don't need to have mathematical knowledge for this. They learn through trial and error when trying to create a tower using blocks and stacking as many blocks as possible before it falls.

## Role-Playing

Role-playing allows parents a chance to be an active part of their child's learning and education. By enacting situations and emotions from books, children can learn the art of storytelling and emotional regulation. Roleplaying also develops empathy and compassion. When they role-play other people, they can experience what it feels like to be in their shoes and learn kindness and acceptance.

## Arts and Crafts Activities

Even a simple activity of making a string of beads can teach them about repetitive patterns, size, shape, and colors. Giving children a chance to witness something more closely and actively is a great way to encourage learning. For example, if they have an assignment where they have to sketch a cityscape, how about a hiking trip to a nearby mountain from where they can have a bird's-eye view of the city? Surely, that will help them with their assignment and make for an amazing trip together.

## Taking the Pause

According to a 2014 study, taking pauses between conversations emphasizes key messages and ideas and allows for better digestion (Thaman & Bachhel, 2014). This practice, although common knowledge, can be used by parents to promote focused and active learning. A two- or three-second pause breaks a lecture or conversation into different sections, boosting attention and increasing the absorption of knowledge. This is also an active learning strategy to help children with revisions, reading, and discussing notes for a project. Those brief seconds of complete silence can help children gather their thoughts better and process the message.

# Conclusion

Children look up to us for guidance, leadership, and advice. Their trust in us is blind. They believe that we can cause them no harm. In return for that devoted trust, it becomes our job to protect them, safeguard their emotions, and ensure they pick up constructive habits from us that lead them to success.

Parental involvement in the education of their child is often an area that gets neglected. They assume that it is the school's job to impart wisdom, prepare them for professional lives, and raise them into sensible, kind, and knowledgeable adults. But not everything can be learned at school alone. Their time there is limited. Furthermore, a teacher has more than one student to teach and educate.

Thus, parental involvement becomes necessary. There are various benefits of it, many of which have been discussed in the book. By becoming engaged in their child's education and well-being, a parent becomes aware of a child's learning style, ability, and pace at which they process new information. By helping them with homework, they can assess their interests and areas of weakness. By going on educational trips, parents can become an active part of their child's learning and expand on what they learn at school. Using active learning techniques, they can make learning more fun and interactive for young children and ensure that they grasp core concepts more firmly.

The "how-to" of all these steps have been talked about in detail along with many activities and practices that parents can use to engage more.

Thank you for giving this book a read. I hope you loved reading it as much as I enjoyed writing it. It would make me the happiest person on earth if you would take a moment to leave an honest review. All you have to do is visit the site where you purchased this book: It's that simple! The review doesn't have to be a full-fledged paragraph; a few words will do. Your few words will help others decide if this is what they should be reading as well. Thank you in advance, and best of luck with your parenting adventures. Every moment is a joyous one with a child.

# References

*10 strategies for schools to improve parent engagement.* (2019, October 5). Getting Smart. https://www.gettingsmart.com/2019/10/05/1 0-strategies-for-schools-to-improve-parent-engagement/

*Active learning.* (2022). Twinkl.com.pk. https://www.twinkl.com.pk/teaching-wiki/active-learning

Barlow, M. (n.d.). *Encouraging active learners in early years settings.* Teach Early Years. https://www.teachearlyyears.com/learning-and-development/view/encouraging-active-learners#:~:text=Active%20learning%20means %20giving%20children

Berkeley Graduate Division. (2019). *Social constructivism | GSI teaching & resource center.* Berkeley.edu. https://gsi.berkeley.edu/gsi-guide-contents/learning-theory-research/social-constructivism/

*Brain Development.* (n.d.). First Things First. https://www.firstthingsfirst.org/early-childhood-matters/brain-development/

Brooks, A. (2019). *Experts discuss the importance of positive parental involvement in education.* Rasmussen.edu. https://www.rasmussen.edu/degrees/education/blog/parental-involvement-in-education/

Cambridge International Education Teaching and Learning Team. (2019). *Getting started with active learning.* Cambridge-Community.org.uk. https://www.cambridge-community.org.uk/professional-development/gswal/index.html

Ceka, A., & Murati, R. (2015). The role of parents in the education of children. *Journal of Education and Practice, 7*(5), 61–64.

Child Crisis AZ. (2017, June 5). *5 important ways fathers impact child development - child crisis.* Child Crisis. https://childcrisisaz.org/5-major-ways-fathers-impact-child-development/

Comer, J. P., & Haynes, N. (1997, July). *The home-school team: An emphasis on parent involvement.* Edutopia; George Lucas Educational Foundation. https://www.edutopia.org/home-school-team

Dearing, E., Kreider, H., Simpkins, S., & Weiss, H. B. (2006). Family involvement in school and low-income children's literacy: Longitudinal associations between and within families. *Journal of Educational Psychology, 98*(4), 653–664. https://doi.org/10.1037/0022-0663.98.4.653

Desforges, C., & Abouchaar, A. (2003). *The impact of parental involvement, parental support and family education on pupil achievements and adjustment: A literature review.* Department for Education and Skills.

Duursma, E., Augustyn, M., & Zuckerman, B. (2008). Reading aloud to children: The evidence. *Archives of Disease in Childhood, 93*(7), 554–557. https://doi.org/10.1136/adc.2006.106336

El Nokali, N. E., Bachman, H. J., & Votruba-Drzal, E. (2010). Parent involvement and children's academic and social development in elementary school. *Child Development, 81*(3), 988–1005. https://doi.org/10.1111/j.1467-8624.2010.01447.x

Emerson, L., Fear, J., Fox, S., & Sanders, E. (2012). *Parental engagement in learning and schooling: Lessons from research.* Australian Research Alliance for Children & Youth for the Family-School and Community Partnerships Bureau.

ÉMWS. (n.d.). Field trips and their importance in a well-rounded education. *Www.ecolemondiale.org.* https://www.ecolemondiale.org/bulletins-board/field-trips-and-their-importance-in-a-well-rounded-education

Fagan, J., & Palkovitz, R. (2007). Unmarried, nonresident fathers' involvement with their infants: A risk and resilience perspective. *Journal*

*of Family Psychology*, *21*(3), 479–489.
https://doi.org/10.1037/0893-3200.21.3.479

Fan, X., & Chen, M. (2001). Parental involvement and students' academic achievement: A meta-analysis. *Educational Psychology Review*, *13*(1), 1–22. https://doi.org/10.1023/a:1009048817385

Freireich, A., & Platzer, B. (2021, March 2). *Don't help your kids with homework*. The Atlantic. https://www.theatlantic.com/education/archiv e/2021/03/right-way-help-kids-homework/618170/

Frost, S. (2009). *Importance of field trips in education | synonym*. Synonym.com. https://classroom.synonym.com/importance-field-trips-education-5438673.html

Gagne, C. (2021, May 8). *Reading to kids: How to raise a book-lover at any age*. Today's Parent. https://www.todaysparent.com/family/reading -to-kids/

*Getting involved at your child's school (for parents)*. (2018, July). Kidshealth.org. https://kidshealth.org/en/parents/school.html

Harris, A. (2005). *Engaging parents in raising achievement do parents know they matter?* https://doi.org/http://dx.doi.org/10.13140/R G.2.1.4902.2965

Henderson, A., & Mapp, K. (2002). *A new wave of evidence the impact of school, family, and community connections on student achievement annual synthesis 2002.* https://sedl.org/connections/resources/eviden ce.pdf

High, P. (2014, June 24). I is for infant: Reading aloud to young children benefits brain development (J. Brown, Interviewer) [Interview]. In *PBS NewsHour.* https://www.pbs.org/newshour/show/infant-reading-aloud-young-children-benefits-brain-development

Hill, N. E., & Tyson, D. F. (2009). Parental involvement in middle school: A meta-analytic assessment of the strategies that promote achievement. *Developmental Psychology, 45*(3), 740–763. https://doi.org/10.1037/a0015362

*How children learn.* (n.d.). Alternatives to School. https://alternativestoschool.com/articles/how-children-learn/

Jurado, B. (2020, February 12). *Ten cool field trip ideas for students of all ages.* Mobile Permissions. https://www.mobilepermissions.com/2020/02 /ten-cool-field-trip-ideas-for-students-of-all-ages/

Kamdar, S. (2021, February 10). *Expert speak: The role of parents in early childhood learning.* Femina.in. https://www.femina.in/relationships/parenting

/expert-speak-the-role-of-parents-in-early-childhood-learning-186062-4.html

Keith, K. L. (2020, December 28). *How parents can be involved with their child's education.* Verywell Family. https://www.verywellfamily.com/parent-involvement-in-schools-619348

Kiser, S. (2020, September 2). *The value of parents helping with homework.* TeachHUB. https://www.teachhub.com/professional-development/2020/09/the-value-of-parents-helping-with-homework/#:~:text=Parental%20involvement%20with%20homework%20and

*Malcolm X quotes about mothers.* (n.d.). A-Z Quotes. Retrieved January 11, 2022, from https://www.azquotes.com/author/9322-Malcolm_X/tag/mother

Marcin, A. (2020, October 14). *Reading to children: Why it's so important and how to start.* Healthline. https://www.healthline.com/health/childrens-health/reading-to-children

Mcleod, S. (2020). *Lev vygotsky's sociocultural theory.* Simply Psychology. https://www.simplypsychology.org/vygotsky.html

McMahon, R. (2017, April 10). *How to raise a reader.* Www.commonsensemedia.org.

https://www.commonsensemedia.org/blog/ho
w-to-raise-a-reader

Murray, A., & Egan, S. M. (2013). Does reading to
infants benefit their cognitive development at 9-
months-old? An investigation using a large birth
cohort survey. *Child Language Teaching and
Therapy*, *30*(3), 303–315.
https://doi.org/10.1177/0265659013513813

National Center on Early Childhood Development,
Teaching and Learning. (n.d.). Read it again!
Benefits of reading to young children. In *Head
Start I ECLKC*.
https://eclkc.ohs.acf.hhs.gov/sites/default/file
s/pdf/read-it-again.pdf

Pontz, E. (2019, April 24). *11 ways parents can get involved
in schools*. Center for Parent and Teen
Communication.
https://parentandteen.com/school-
involvement/

PTA, N. (2000). *Building successful partnerships : A guide for
developing parent and family involvement programs*.
National Education Service.

Rizzolo, D., Zipp, G. P., Stiskal, D., & Simpkins, S.
(2011). Stress management strategies for
students: The immediate effects of yoga,
humor, and reading on stress. *Journal of College
Teaching & Learning (TLC)*, *6*(8).
https://doi.org/10.19030/tlc.v6i8.1117

Sethna, V., Perry, E., Domoney, J., Iles, J., Psychogiou, L., Rowbotham, N. E. L., Stein, A., Murray, L., & Ramchandani, P. G. (2017). Father–child interactions at 3 months and 24 months: Contributions to children's cognitive development at 24 months. *Infant Mental Health Journal*, *38*(3), 378–390. https://doi.org/10.1002/imhj.21642

Sheldon, S. B., & Jung, S. B. (2015). *The family engagement partnership student outcome evaluation*. Flamboyan Foundation.

*Should parents help with homework: The pros and cons*. (2021, April 23). Assign U. https://assignu.com/homework/should-parents-help-with-homework/

Singh, A. (2020, June 23). *How to make child an active learner*. The Asian School. https://www.theasianschool.net/blog/how-to-make-child-an-active-learner/

Stambor, Z. (2005, December). Meet the renaissance dad. *Monitor*, 62. American Psychological Association. https://www.apa.org/monitor/dec05/renaissance

Stephen. (2019, April 2). *Educational family trip | the importance & place to go*. Educational School Trips. https://www.educationalschooltrip.com/educat

ional-family-trip-importance-place-to-
go/#:~:text=The%20Importance%20of%20Ed
ucational%20Family%20Trip&text=Family%20
vacations%20are%20not%20just

Stuart, H. (2018, November 6). *The top 4 educational benefits of school trips.* Www.easchooltours.com. https://www.easchooltours.com/blog/the-educational-benefits-of-school-field-trips-for-student-learning

Thaman, R. G., & Bachhel, R. (2014). Effective use of pause procedure to enhance student engagement and learning. *Journal of Clinical and Diagnostic Research*, *8*(8), XM01–XM03. https://doi.org/10.7860/jcdr/2014/8260.4691

*The benefits of reading together as a family.* (2020, November 17). Familius.com Shop. https://www.familius.com/benefits-of-reading-together-as-a-family/

*The importance of reading together • new york city children's theater.* (2017, August 3). Https://Www.nycchildrenstheater.org/. https://www.nycchildrenstheater.org/2017/08/the-importance-of-reading-together/#:~:text=Reading%20together%20is%20an%20activity

UKEssays. (2018, November). *The role of parents in school education essay.* UKEssays.com. https://www.ukessays.com/essays/education/t

he-role-of-parents-in-school-education-essay.php

Veerendra. (2020, April 28). *Role of parents in education.* A plus Topper. https://www.aplustopper.com/role-of-parents-in-education/

Wairimu, M. J., Macharia, S. M., & Muiru, A. (2016). Analysis of parental involvement and self-esteem on secondary school students in kieni west sub-county, nyeri county, kenya. *Journal of Education and Practice,* *7*(27). https://www.semanticscholar.org/paper/Analysis-of-Parental-Involvement-And-Self-Esteem-On-Wairimu-Macharia/b3f74b1be8b4a2135ed7178692cbeca3391b05e4

Waterford. (2018, November 1). *How parent involvement leads to student success | waterford.org.* Waterford.org. https://www.waterford.org/education/how-parent-involvment-leads-to-student-success/

*What is active learning in early childhood.* (2021, August 10). Edge Early Learning. https://edgeearlylearning.com.au/what-is-active-learning-in-early-childhood/